BASEBALL

CONSULTANTS

Dick Siebert
Baseball Coach,
University of Minnesota

Otto Vogel
Baseball Coach,
University of Iowa

ATHLETIC INSTITUTE SERIES

STERLING PUBLISHING CO., Inc.   New York

Foreword

"Baseball" is but one item in a comprehensive list of sports instruction aids made available on a non-profit basis by The Athletic Institute. The photographic material in this book has been reproduced in total from The Athletic Institute's sound, color slidefilm, "Beginning Baseball." This book and the slidefilm are parts of a program designed to bring the many benefits of athletics, physical education and recreation to everyone.

The Athletic Institute is a non-profit organization devoted to the advancement of athletics, physical education and recreation. It functions on the premise that athletics and recreation bring benefits of inestimable value to the individual and to the community.

The nature and scope of the many Institute programs are determined by an advisory committee of selected persons noted for their outstanding knowledge, experience and ability in the fields of athletics, physical education and recreation.

It is their hope, and the hope of the Institute, that through this book, the reader will become a better baseball player, skilled in the fundamentals of this fine game. Knowledge, and the practice necessary to mold knowledge into playing ability, are the keys to real enjoyment of playing baseball.

Second Printing, 1966

Copyright © 1965 by The Athletic Institute
Published by Sterling Publishing Co., Inc.
419 Park Avenue South, New York, N.Y. 10016
All rights reserved
Manufactured in the United States of America
Library of Congress Catalog Card No.: 65-15814

CONTENTS

TYPICAL BASEBALL INFIELD LAYOUT

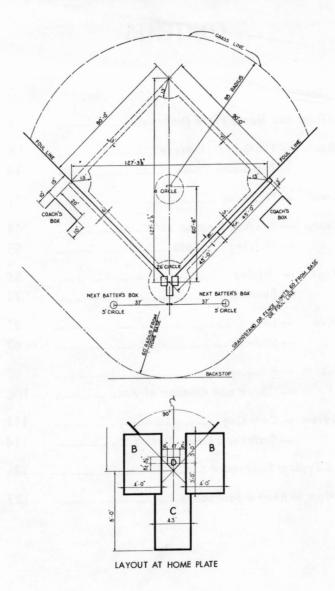

LAYOUT AT HOME PLATE

HISTORY

In old colonial days the aristocracy of young New York spent their leisure hours playing or watching a game of cricket, brought from England by the settlers.

At the same time the people of Boston were playing a somewhat similar game called "rounders." These two imported games, cricket and rounders, were the joint ancestors of the great American game of baseball.

The colonial youngsters actually started the development. When they wanted to play they had to make their own equipment out of whatever materials they could find.

And with the same originality, they made their own rules. They took the rules of rounders and roughened them up a bit.

One player, known as the "feeder," would toss the ball to the striker, underhand and slowly, to be sure he hit it.

The "striker" would hit it as far as he could and then try to run to a nearby stump or stake and back before . . .

. . . either the "feeder" or the "scout" could retrieve the ball and throw it with all his force . . .

. . . to hit the runner before he could reach home. This was the rowdy, simple game that eventually became baseball.

As more people joined the game, they simply set out more stakes around which the "striker" had to run before getting back "home." The youngsters called their game "Town Ball."

Here is what the Town Ball field looked like. Already, it was developing toward a baseball diamond as we know it today.

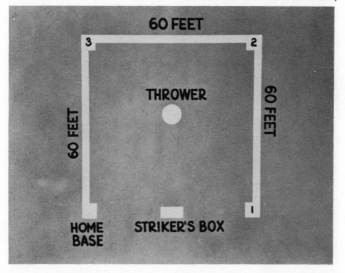

60 FEET

3   2

THROWER

60 FEET

60 FEET

1

HOME BASE   STRIKER'S BOX

9

Meanwhile, back in New York, the former cricket enthusiasts were developing their game in a somewhat similar direction. Instead of wickets they had developed a game with four bases. They called their game "The New York Game."

And here's what their field looked like. They too were developing the game toward the modern baseball idea.

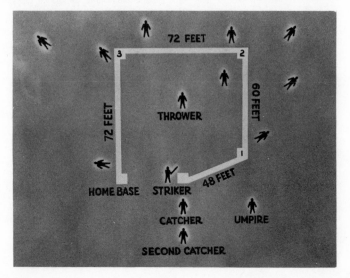

Then one day, in 1845, a young surveyor named Alexander Cartwright gave the orderly touch of the draftsman to developing the game. He designed the first baseball diamond.

On a field in Hoboken, New Jersey, in 1846, the new game got its trial in a match between the New York Nine and the Knickerbocker Club. By the new rules there were nine men on a team. A turn at bat was called a "hand" and a circuit of the bases was called an "ace." The first team to score twenty-one aces won the game.

The ball was made of hard, solid rubber . . . as lively as a tennis ball . . . but as hard on the hands as a present day baseball.

The bat had a broad, flat hitting side. It wasn't too difficult to hit the ball with a bat as broad as that, particularly . . .

. . . since the thrower didn't really pitch. His job was to feed the ball to the striker and make it easy for him to hit it.

The game increased steadily in popularity. When the Civil War shifted the population and mingled together men from all the States, many a northeastern soldier carried the equipment of the New York Game with him.

They played whenever they could. Westerners learned the game from Easterners and southern prisoners in northern camps were fascinated as they watched. Here was a game with an appeal that cut through sectional differences . . . a game that found response in the basic Americanism of both armies . . . a sport that seemed to strike a key chord in the spirit of the new country. The returning veterans took the game home with them.

Soon every hamlet in every state had its ball team. Teams visited for matches, and a match with the team from a neighboring town was the occasion for a complete local holiday and an all-day celebration. The players were the heroes of the hour . . . if they won. Americans were taking baseball to their hearts.

The rules, equipment and playing technique were steadily improving to make the game one of skill and stamina. The easy cricket style was disappearing.

The pitcher really pitched with all his speed and cunning. Now his object was to prevent the batter from hitting, if possible.

The batter used a round bat now and found it considerably harder to handle then the flat cricket bat.

A part of the gallantry of the game was the noble catcher who lasted nine innings and still disdained to wear either glove or mask, even though he caught the ball on the first bounce. The ninth inning often found him battered but unbowed.

Soon, amid the jeers of the he-man players, catchers started to wear tight gloves, flesh colored, hoping not to be noticed. But, they were noticed, so, finally . . .

. . . one courageous catcher faced the crowd wearing not only a padded mitt, but a mask as well. Now, he could move up and catch the ball before it bounced. Baseball was becoming a game of skill and you can't be skilled with a bloody nose and raw hands.

Soon, the rest of the team adopted protective equipment and ever since then baseball has developed steadily in speed, skill and precision until . . .

. . . today baseball has taken a grip on the imagination of Americans everywhere. It has become a national institution, America's national game.

Today's regulation baseball is a very different ball from the hard rubber sphere of the New York Game. Now it has a cork or rubber center with a tight wool winding and a horsehide cover.

Today, every player, regardless of his playing position, wears a mitt or a glove. Although the rules of the game prescribe certain weights and sizes for this equipment, there is a wide variety of styles . . . each style having been carefully designed and manufactured to increase the players' skill.

The once bloody but unbowed catcher is now protected fully by a mask, a chest protector and shin guards. As a key member of the team his equipment is designed to allow freedom of action as well as to provide protection.

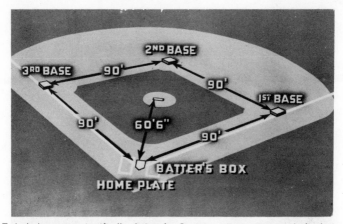

Today's bats are scientifically designed and standardized in various sizes, every one shaped and balanced accurately to suit the size, strength and hitting style of the player.

Strange as it may seem, today's playing field is not greatly different from Alexander Cartwright's original design. Still diamond shaped, it has remained ninety feet on all sides.

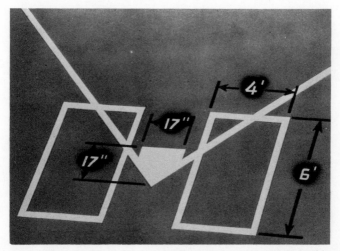

Lines extending straight out from home plate beyond first and third base separate fair from foul territory.

The batter's box on either side of home plate, is four feet by six feet. Home plate itself is 17 inches wide and 17 inches from the front to the back corner.

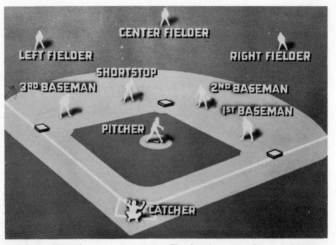

The pitcher and catcher, as a pair, are known as "the battery." The distance from the front of the pitcher's plate to the back corner of home plate is sixty feet, six inches.

The first baseman, the second baseman, the shortstop and the third baseman are known as infielders.

Completing the nine-man team and known as the outfielders are the right fielder, the center fielder and the left fielder.

To understand how skilled baseball has become since the days of Town Ball and the New York Game, let's examine a few facts.

The pitcher must pitch the ball with all his speed and trickery to try to prevent the batter from hitting it and still make it pass through the strike zone which is only as wide as home plate and between the batter's shoulders and just below his knee-caps.

With the pitched ball traveling as fast as ninety miles an hour, the batter has less than half a second to decide whether or not to try to hit it.

After he has decided, he still has to use part of that half second to get the bat around and meet the ball in exactly the right place. Actually the ball is within the reach of his bat for only 1/50th of a second. This makes it easier to understand why hitting takes a keen eye, good judgment, a fine sense of timing and well controlled strength.

After hitting the ball, the batter must run to first base as fast as he can. A good runner can make it in less than four seconds. And in that short time, the whole defensive strategy of the opposing team goes into action.

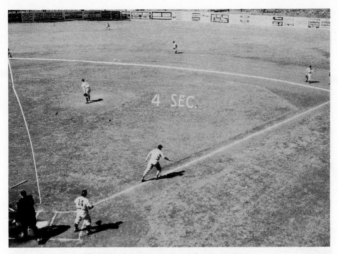

In that four seconds, while the runner runs ninety feet, the defensive team must get the ball over to first base. Four seconds—that's one — two — three — four. That's all it takes for a play in baseball.

Most of the time the fielder can't even take time to straighten up to throw. Without wasting a fraction of a second he must get it to first base. But that's not all.

His throw should be so accurate that the first baseman doesn't have to take his foot off the base to catch the ball. In close decisions at first base, those split seconds make all the difference between defeat and victory.

When a runner tries to steal second, it's the catcher who has some split second work to do. The runner starts with the pitch.

Now the catcher has less than three seconds to catch the ball and to throw it down to second base ahead of the runner.

And over that distance, about 130 feet, his throw has to be so accurate that the second baseman can catch it right down near the base to save those precious split parts of a second it would take him to bring down a higher throw.

25

Through all the excitement of a game the catcher must keep his composure and be the calm strategist of the game, signalling every pitch, watching every play position and planning the defensive strategy, play by play.

When all of these factors are realized it's easy to understand that modern baseball is a game of finely developed skill, trained, accurate judgment, speed of both mind and body and the strength of well disciplined muscles. In a young player, all of these abilities can be developed through two basic steps . . .

. . . first, a sure knowledge of the fundamentals of individual skills, and then . . . steady, consistent, week-in, week-out practice . . . practice that stresses the fundamentals of the game.

2

THROWING

If any single skill in baseball is more important than all others, that skill is throwing.

Unless every man on the team can throw accurately and with speed enough to beat a runner from whatever position he plays, the team cannot be strong on defense. The man who cannot throw well weakens his team defensively.

There are three types of throws. This is an underhand throw, used only when it's important to get the ball away fast and there isn't time to straighten up.

This sidearm throw is good for short, quick throws, but it should be used only in emergencies by most ball players.

By far the most used and most valuable throw is this overhand throw. It is more accurate and has more carry than any other type of throw. This is the throw for power and control.

A beginning ball player is wise to learn the overhand throw first, then practice it until all the fundamentals are natural and he has achieved speed and control. Then the other two throws develop naturally.

Your grip on the ball is the biggest factor in control, so you should adopt the correct grip at the very start and use the

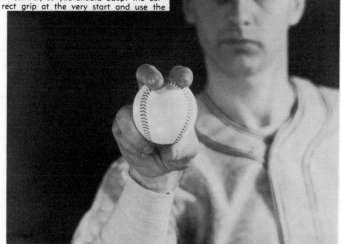

same grip on every throw. Even in practice, never vary your grip. The feel of the ball is so important that you should never practice with anything but a regulation baseball—certainly never with a tennis ball or any other kind of ball.

There is the correct grip—the ball held between your thumb and first two fingers, with your third finger resting lightly against the ball. Two fingers slightly spread on top—thumb on bottom, directly below the fingers.

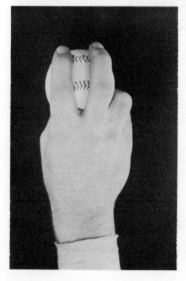

There's what the correct grip looks like from your own view. Preferably your first two fingers should grip across the seam, because this gives you better control and helps you put spin on the ball.

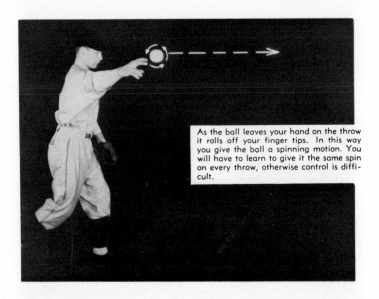

As the ball leaves your hand on the throw it rolls off your finger tips. In this way you give the ball a spinning motion. You will have to learn to give it the same spin on every throw, otherwise control is difficult.

Let's analyze the fundamentals of the throwing movement. As your arm comes forward in the throw, your upper arm and forearm form an approximate right angle, the upper arm about parallel with the ground.

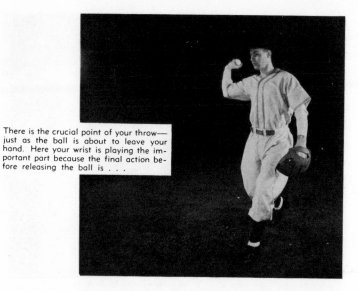

There is the crucial point of your throw—just as the ball is about to leave your hand. Here your wrist is playing the important part because the final action before releasing the ball is . . .

. . . a snap of the wrist that gives the throw your last ounce of power. This snap action is an essential part of every throw and it can make or break you as a defensive ball player. So let's learn it first.

Practice the snap alone for a while. Stand in the release position . . . body upright . . . upper arm straight out from the shoulder . . . forearm vertical, and lay your wrist back as far as it will go without taking your forearm back with it.

Now, from here, throw the ball without moving any part of your body except your wrist and hand.

Just snap your hand forward from the wrist with all the power you can put into it, and throw the ball as far and as straight as you can. Practice this snap for a while and you'll feel your wrist settling down into an easy, rhythmic throw.

32

Now let's add more power by putting some arm into the throw. Keep your body erect and lay your whole arm back as far as it will go, still keeping your upper arm approximately parallel with the ground.

Keep the right angle at your elbow and stretch your arm back until you can feel the pull across your chest. Arm back from shoulder . . . forearm laid back from the elbow . . . hand laid back on the wrist—back as far as they will go.

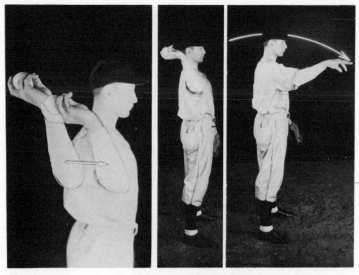

The movement starts in your shoulder as you start bringing your arm forward like a whip. Your elbow leads the movement first, and as your upper arm comes forward, your forearm stays laid back and your wrist tends to lay back still farther.

When the forward movement brings your elbow up even with your shoulder as in the left picture, the whip action continues on through as your forearm, wrist and hand snap the ball forward from the release position. Then the whole arm follows through.

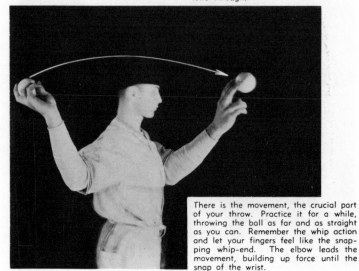

There is the movement, the crucial part of your throw. Practice it for a while, throwing the ball as far and as straight as you can. Remember the whip action and let your fingers feel like the snapping whip-end. The elbow leads the movement, building up force until the snap of the wrist.

Movement of your body adds the maxi-
mum power to your throw. So let's
analyze the basic body movements to
complete the full throw.

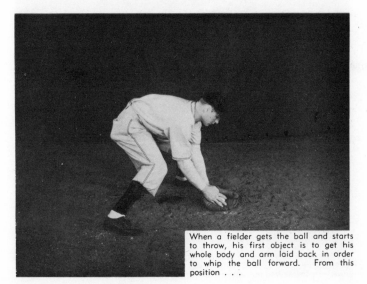

When a fielder gets the ball and starts
to throw, his first object is to get his
whole body and arm laid back in order
to whip the ball forward. From this
position . . .

. . . the weight shifts immediately to the back foot as the throwing arm swings backward toward the full layback posi-tion. At the same time the body is swinging back until . . .

. . . in the full layback position, your weight is fully on your rear foot and your body and throwing arm are stretched backward, reaching back to get as much power as possible into the forward throw.

Simultaneous with the backward move-ment of the throwing arm and body, your front foot starts forward toward the target.

There is the movement. From the fielding position, your throwing arm and body are stretched backward like an extended whip, ready to snap forward in the throw. There is a momentary pause in the lay-back position. Then . . .

. . . your forward foot completes its stride and your body starts moving forward. As your weight comes onto your front foot, your front leg braces to act as a firm support for the throw, your forward foot pointing toward the target.

As your forward leg braces, your hips thrust forward and pivot around square with the target, your whole body moving forward against your braced front leg. As your body comes forward . . .

. . . the whiplike movement goes on through your shoulder into your arms and ends in a snap of the wrist as you release the ball. The arm movement is exactly as you practiced it earlier. All the power of your body, from your feet through your legs, hips, back, shoulders and arm to your wrist has been built up, and now . . .

. . . it is all released as you let the ball
go. But your movement does not stop
here. Your whole body follows through.
Throw your hand forward after the ball.

Your arm keeps on moving in a full follow-through.

Let your body swing around naturally on
your forward foot as your back leg swings
around into a balanced position.

There is the basic throw of baseball . . .
a whiplike movement from a full layback
to a full free follow-through after the
ball. These basic fundamentals apply to
all throws.

Infielders do not often have time for a
full overhand throw, so they get the ball
away faster with a snap overhand throw.
From the fielding position they get into
throwing position as fast as possible,
bringing their throwing arm up to the
layback position the shortest and fastest
way. From this point the throw is very
similar to the full overhand throw.

The throwing movement is the same sequence of forward movements. The stride toward the target and then the whipping movement that ends in the wrist to snap the ball forward . . . then a normal follow-through.

The sidearm throw is another throw an infielder may use in special situations.

The only difference between the full sidearm and the overhand throw is that in the full sidearm the arm is held out to the side with less bend in the elbow throughout the swing and the body pivots more. The whiplike movement that ends with a snap of the wrist as the ball is released and the follow-through is the same as in all other throws.

For shorter, quicker throws the sidearm snap throw may be used. The sidearm snap follows all the fundamental movements of the snap overhand. From the fielding position in the left picture, bring the ball back to the layback position the shortest, fastest way. Then snap the ball forward as in the right picture.

On certain plays this underhand snap throw can be used. Here is the movement, containing the same fundamentals of all other throws but the body does not straighten up.

Throwing is one of the most important basic skills of baseball and skill at throwing is every man's obligation to the team. But throwing is not necessarily a natural ability. A good throwing arm can be acquired by consistent practice and careful observance of these fundamentals.

3

FIELDING

Fielding is a responsibility of every man on the team no matter what position he plays. Every player of a winning team must be able to field both ground balls and fly balls.

Like all the other positions and skills of baseball, skill at fielding is a combination of natural ability and constant practice in the fundamentals of the fielding movements.

Here is the basic fielding position to use while you are learning to field ground balls. Keep low—close to the ground— so close that your hands touch the ground when hanging naturally. It's easier to come up after a ball than drop down for it, so KEEP LOW FOR GROUND BALLS.

44

Ready to field a ball, your heels are approximately together, weight on the balls of your feet, knees turned outward, body bent slightly forward, eyes on the ball. The palms are turned outward, little fingers together, fingers downward. To get the feel of fielding, take this position and have someone roll a ball to you.

Let the ball roll into your glove and, as it does, your throwing hand rolls over and traps it in the glove. After you have learned to field a ground ball in this manner, you are ready to advance to the fielding position for normal play.

There is your position waiting for the pitch, facing the batter, eyes on the pitcher, watching for the ball, feet comfortably spread, knees slightly bent, weight slightly forward.

As the ball is pitched, shift your weight slightly forward so that you will be able to get a fast start in any direction. If the ball is hit in your direction, you'll have to get in front of it as fast as you can.

If the ball is hit fairly hard and directly at you, come in on the ball if you have time. Play the ball. Don't let it play you.

As the ball nears, you set yourself in fielding position, feet comfortably spread, right foot slightly behind the left, body low with knees well bent, back fairly straight and eyes "glued" on the ball. This position may be assumed after you have learned to field the ball properly from the basic fielding position.

Keep your eyes on the ball as it settles into the glove; then bring your throwing hand over it to trap it securely.

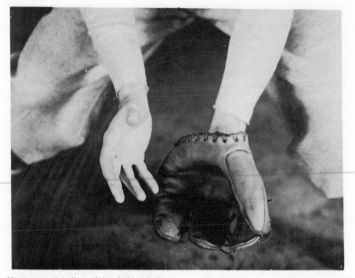

Most ground balls will be fielded below the belt, which means that the fingers will be pointing downward, palms facing the ball and your little fingers close together.

Sometimes a ball will hop high and above the belt. In this case your fingers will be pointing upward, palms once more facing the ball and your thumbs close together.

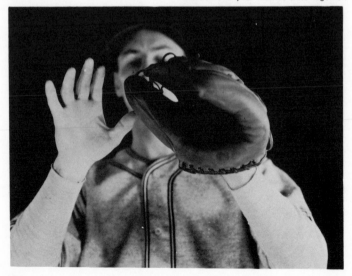

These are the two basic positions for learning how to field ground balls. Practice these fundamental fielding positions by having someone hit balls straight to you.

On slow ground balls hit directly at you, you must come in fast keeping the body low. Then place the glove on the ground well in front of you and allow the ball to roll into it, clasping it immediately with the throwing hand.

In case the play must be made in a hurry, it might even be necessary for you to pick up the ball with the bare hand. In this case, field the ball in front of the right foot with the body to the left of the ball. This should not be attempted however until you have become an adept fielder.

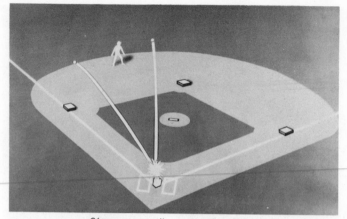

Of course, not all ground balls are hit
directly at the fielder. Some are hit to
the left, some to the right. As a fielder
you must get in front of the ball as fast
as you can.

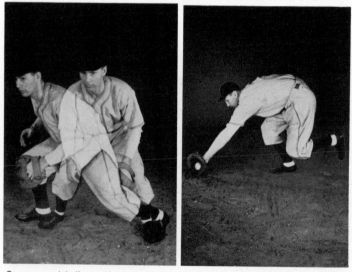

On a ground ball to either side, don't
think you have lots of time. Turn in the
direction of the ball immediately and get
in front of it as fast as possible. Don't
straighten up. Keep your body low. Here
the fielder is going for a ground ball to
his right.

During your run keep your eye on the
ball. Never let it get out of your eye
focus until you have it in your glove, even
if you must field the ball from this
position.

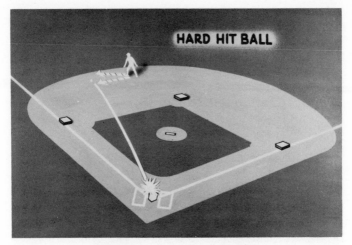

The direction of your run will depend on how hard the ball has been hit. Here is a hard hit ball to the right of the fielder. The fielder should cut straight across or diagonally back to meet it.

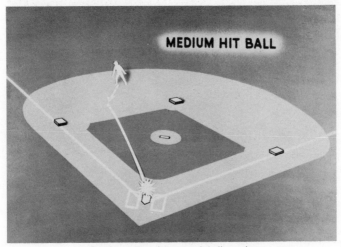

For a medium hit ground ball to the right of the fielder, he should run diagonally forward toward the ball.

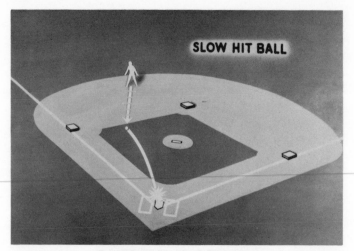

SLOW HIT BALL

For a slow hit ball to the fielder's right, he should come in fast and straighter toward the ball. The important thing in direction is to judge the speed of the ball and get in front of it as soon as possible.

Most throws by infielders are to their left. If you're running for a ground ball to your right, you'll have to stop and get set for a throw in the opposite direction. In this case . . .

. . . stop squarely in front of the ball by jamming your right foot against the ground. Field the ball with your legs apart, your right leg braced.

Your braced leg, jammed against the ground, gives you a firm support for your throw back to your left.

If you have to run to the left for a ground ball, and do not have time to get in front of it and get set for the throw, then . . .

. . . check your momentum as quickly as possible, making the throw off the right foot and stepping in the direction of the throw with your left. Here the fielder fields the ball with his left foot forward.

The step with the right foot checks the run. Then a pivot on the right foot and a step toward first base with the left foot for the throw.

Here is an important point. When you get the ball in your glove, don't rush the throw unnecessarily. Set yourself for an overhand throw, then give it everything you have.

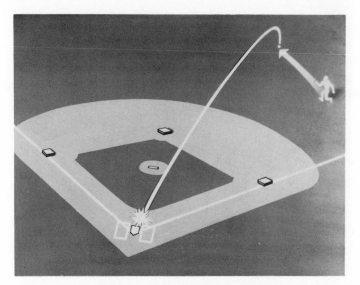

On all fly balls there is one cardinal rule for fielders—GET UNDER IT FAST. GET UNDER IT AND WAIT.

For a fly ball hit either to his right or left, a fielder should be able to turn in that direction quickly, with whatever footwork proves fastest for him. For a fly ball hit straight over his head there is another factor that determines which way he should turn.

That factor is wind direction. No fielder should start an inning without first checking the direction of the wind.

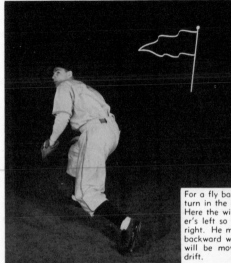

For a fly ball hit straight over your head, turn in the direction the wind is blowing. Here the wind is blowing from the fielder's left so the ball will drift toward his right. He makes his first step diagonally backward with the right foot so that he will be moving in the direction of the drift.

Try to determine approximately where the ball will fall. Then turn and run to that spot. Never run backward if you can avoid it. Turn around and run after the ball, glancing over your shoulder as you run.

Get under the ball as soon as you can . . . get set . . . and wait for it. Don't reach for the ball until you are under it. There are two positions for your hands while catching fly balls.

You can hold your hands like this, with
your little fingers together . . .

. . . or like this, with your thumbs together. Through practice you will be able
to make an instinctive decision about the
position of your hands on every fly ball.

Let the ball drop into your gloved hand and immediately trap it with the other. Then get the ball into the infield as fast as you can.

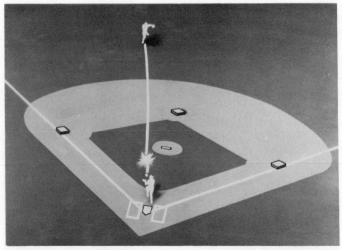

If you make an exceptionally long throw, such as to home plate, throw the ball to about thirty feet in front of its target and let it hop the rest of the way. This will eliminate overthrows and, in case of a throw to home plate, the ball can be handled for a cut-off, if necessary.

What you have learned so far are only the basic fundamentals of fielding. If you learn these fundamentals and practice them until all the correct movements are instinctive with you. you will be capable of the alert, skilled fielding that wins ball games.

4

HITTING

Successful hitting skill is a combination of three factors—natural ability, confidence and the use of the basic fundamentals.

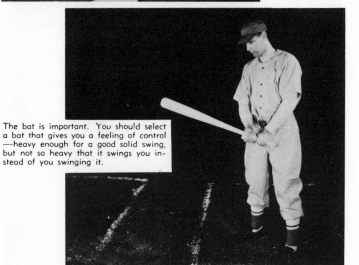

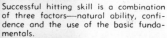

The bat is important. You should select a bat that gives you a feeling of control —heavy enough for a good solid swing, but not so heavy that it swings you instead of you swinging it.

In the correct grip your hands may be together or only slightly spread, gripping from opposite sides with fingers and thumbs wrapped well around the handle.

If you turn your hands up and look at the backs, you should see your knuckles in approximately this position. The second knuckles of your upper hand are lined up somewhere between the base knuckles and the second knuckles of your lower hand.

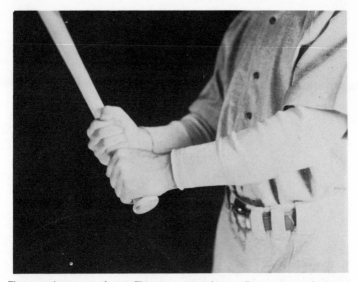

There are three types of grip. This one, called the end grip, with the hands down close to the knob of the bat, is used by power hitters who want to get the leverage of the full bat length into their swing.

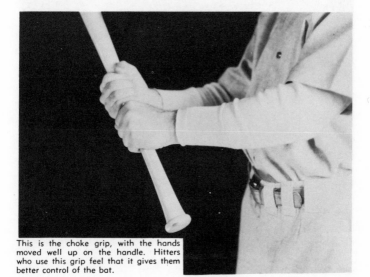

This is the choke grip, with the hands moved well up on the handle. Hitters who use this grip feel that it gives them better control of the bat.

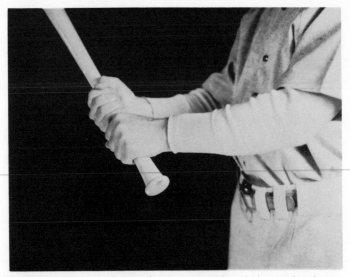

This modified grip, with the lower hand an inch or two from the knob, is by far the most popular, because hitters feel that it gives them both control and power. Through most of the swing the grip is firm but relaxed.

In taking your stance, stand just far enough away from the plate so that you can grip the bat with either hand and touch the outside corner of the plate by bending over only slightly. In the placement of the feet there are three basic types of stance.

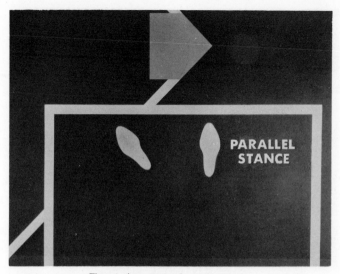

There is the position of your feet in what is called the parallel stance. Both feet approximately the same distance from the plate.

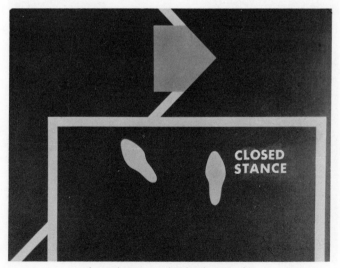

In another stance, the closed stance, the front foot is closer to the plate than the rear foot.

63

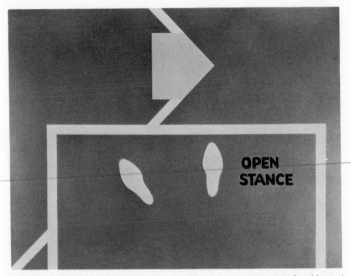

OPEN
STANCE

In the third basic stance, the open stance, the front foot is farther away from the plate. For beginning hitters let's concentrate on the parallel stance. As you de- velop your own most comfortable posi- tion, you can adapt your stance to either a more closed or a more open stance.

Place your feet in the correct parallel stance position, comfortably spread, front foot turned slightly toward the pitcher.

Now let's analyze the ready-to-hit posi- tion, just as the pitcher is ready to de- liver the ball.

Your knees should not be locked. Relax them. The important thing is to feel comfortable.

Hips should be relaxed too—square with the plate and parallel with the feet.

Your arms should be comfortably away from the body and bent at the elbows. The forward arm guides the swing so the forearm should be kept almost parallel with the ground.

The back arm puts the power into the swing so it can drop a little into a comfortable position. Don't drop it too far and don't pin it against your body. It must be free to move. Shoulders should be as level as possible. Your head should be firm and steady, eyes on the ball and ready to follow it as long as possible from the time the pitcher starts his delivery.

This is your ready-to-hit position—firm, steady, comfortable, relaxed. But keep the bat off your shoulder. It should be held well back at an angle about half way between the vertical and the horizontal. Now you're ready for the swing.

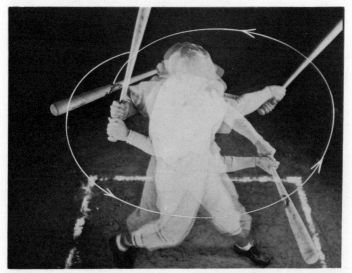

The hitting swing is actually a powerful coiling and uncoiling of the hips, shoulders and arms around a central axis, which is the backbone. A rhythmic timing of a progressive movement that starts with a pivot of the hips and shoulders, flowing through the arms and wrists, gathering power as it goes and continuing to a full follow-through.

The swing starts as the pitcher delivers the ball. The weight shifts back to the rear foot and at the same time the front foot reaches forward in a glide to meet the pitch. The glide should be natural—neither too long nor too short. Simultaneously . . .

. . . the hips, shoulders, arms and bat pivot back around the backbone axis. This pivot carries the bat even further back. Now your weight is all on your back foot and your body and arms are tightly coiled around your backbone.

A quick push off the inside of the back foot starts the uncoiling movement. As the forward foot hits the ground, the whole front leg braces. The forward pivot of the hips has just started, and from this point on you swing against the braced front leg.

The timing of the swing is such that your hands are well in front of the body before the bat is squared around to meet the ball. The weight of the body is all on the forward foot and the whole left side is firm just before the ball reaches the hitting zone. At this point your wrists come into action.

As you swing the bat toward the ball your wrists and hands are in the position of the picture on the left. As your bat contacts the ball the wrists snap. Then they roll over into the position in the right picture.

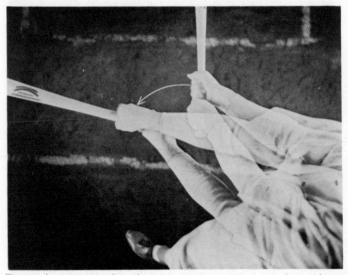

There is the wrist action from the snap to the roll-over. First the snap as your bat contacts the ball. Then the roll-over as you continue around toward your follow-through.

Simultaneously with this wrist snap, your back hip goes into the ball and your forward hip is thrown out of the way. Now, the ball has been hit but you are still swinging. Don't stop here.

The back foot pivots in on the ball of the foot until the heel lifts off the ground. The toe stays on the ground to keep your balance. The bat is still swinging.

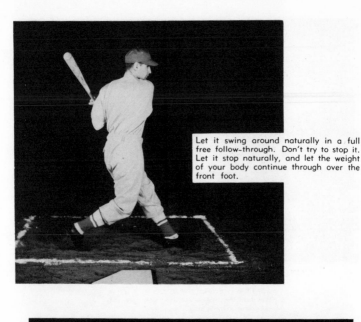

Let it swing around naturally in a full free follow-through. Don't try to stop it. Let it stop naturally, and let the weight of your body continue through over the front foot.

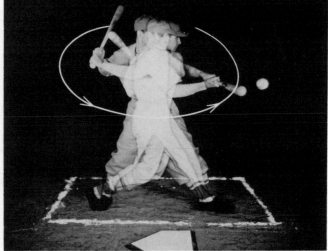

There's the swing,—a controlled, powerful movement of all your muscles to swing the bat through a flat arc. A coiling and uncoiling of your body and arms around your backbone, building up power to be released all together at the exact instant your bat hits the ball. Practice this swing, making sure you follow all the fundamentals, and you stand a good chance of becoming a high average hitter.

Bunting is an entirely separate phase of
hitting and uses altogether different
fundamentals. There are two types of
bunts—the sacrifice bunt and the bunt
for a base hit.

The sacrifice bunt is used to advance a
runner already on a base and, since the
opposition usually expects it, this bunt is
made with the whole body square to the
pitcher.

73

The shift from normal ready-to-hit stance to the sacrifice bunting stance is made just before the pitcher releases the ball.

There are two methods of making this shift.

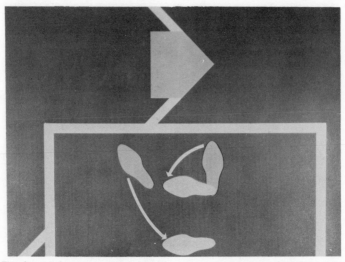

The first method requires the shift of only one foot. If you stand close to the plate like this . . .

. . . you pivot on your back foot until it points toward the pitcher and swing your front foot back even with it in a comfortable stance.

74

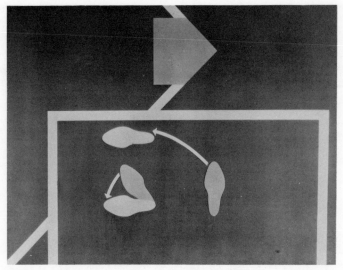

If you stand farther away from the plate like this . . .

. . . you should pivot on your front foot and swing your back foot up even with it.

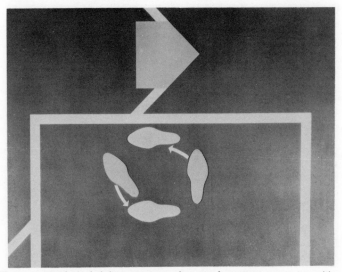

The second method of shifting requires the movement of both feet. The front foot moves back away from the plate and

the rear foot moves up to a position even with the front foot.

Here is the movement. From the ready-to-hit position, the front foot has moved into the position of the left picture. Then the rear foot moves up parallel with the front foot, as in the picture on the right.

Regardless of which method of shifting you use, the fundamentals of bunting are the same. As you pivot, slide your upper hand up on the bat to a position close to the trade mark. The lower hand remains steady and firm.

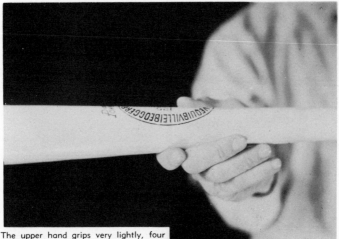

The upper hand grips very lightly, four fingers underneath and thumb on top. The grip is so light with this hand that the bat just rests on the fingers.

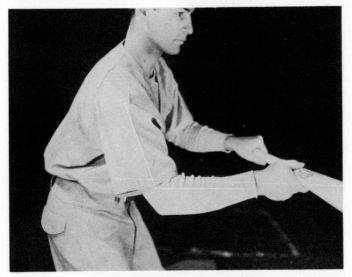

The forearm of the forward arm should be approximately parallel with the ground and the angle between the forearm and upper arm should be approximately a right angle.

There is your correct bunting position for a sacrifice bunt. Body slightly crouched, head up, eyes on the ball . . . weight slightly forward, arms relaxed and bent at the elbows, holding the bat parallel to the ground. Now you're ready to bunt.

As the ball approaches, try to keep the bat as level as possible. Get the bat in front of the ball by lowering or raising your body from your knees and waist. Move your arms as little as possible.

Let the ball hit the bat. As the ball hits, the bat will recoil into the "V" between the thumb and forefinger of your upper hand. This deadens the impact and prevents the ball from bouncing too far.

In the second type of bunt—the bunt for a base hit—deception is important, so you shift your feet as little as possible.

After the pitcher has delivered the ball, simply step toward the pitch with your forward foot and bring your bat into bunting position.

The bunting technique is the same as in the sacrifice bunt. Your rear hand holds firm. Your forward hand holds the bat loosely, and as the ball strikes the bat, the bat recoils back into the forward hand.

A hitter is the prized member of every team. Whether he is a careful accurate bunter who can put them where he wants them or . . .

. . . the heavy hitter who knocks them out of the park, every batter must know all these fundamentals of hitting and bunting. He must practice them carefully until the pattern of the swing and bunt is natural to him. Then he's a power on any team. Remember, all good hitters have their individual styles, but a consistently good hitter never violates certain basic fundamentals.

5

BASE RUNNING

There is a one word motto for base runners. It's "HUSTLE." When you hit . . . when the third strike or fourth ball gets by the catcher . . . HUSTLE. Hustle on everything and never assume that the throw will beat you until the umpire says you're out.

After the hit, you don't measure time in seconds any more—it's split seconds to beat out the throw to first, and you can save precious time by getting a good start.

The swing of a right-handed hitter carries him around and away from first base. He can best get his start by . . .

. . . pushing off with his left foot and
throwing his body in the direction of first
base. The left foot starts the drive.

The first step comes with the right foot,
and from there on it's a straight run
down the base line.

A left-handed hitter swings around toward
first base and his follow-through sets his
momentum in that direction. He can
capitalize on that advantage by . . .

. . . pushing off on the ball of his right
foot and leaning his body in the direction
of his run.

A left-handed hitter takes his first step
with his left foot.

During the run to first base, if your hit
is to the right side of the diamond, you
can easily tell what's happening to the
ball. If your hit is to the left side, a
quick glance over your shoulder without
slackening speed will help you decide
what to do at first base.

84

If it looks as though it will be close at first, take a straight line to the bag, just a little to the right of the foul line, and don't try to stop. Run straight through along the right field line and . . .

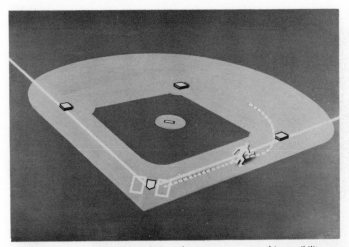

. . . don't let up speed until you have touched the bag.

As you approach first base you may see the possibility of advancing to second.

As soon as you see this possibility, you should swing out to the right to start a flat arc that will cut the inside corner of first base and continue in an easy curve toward second.

Here's how you start that arc coming down the first base line. Start by leaning your weight slightly to the right and taking a couple of steps at an angle into foul territory.

As you round the bag try to hit the inside corner with whichever foot is most convenient in your stride. Don't try to hit the bag with a certain foot. Let your stride take care of it.

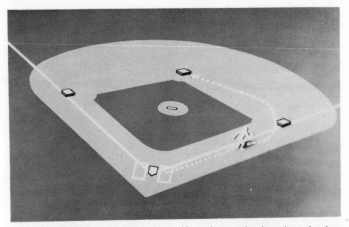

The run from first, through second, third and home is merely a continuation of the same flat arc you started at first base. If you have to hustle to beat the throw into second, that arc should straighten out as you take the shortest possible route to the base.

It the play is very close at second, you should slide. Sliding is a skill that can be acquired fairly easily. In learning though, remember that there is one fundamental rule — IF YOU DECIDE TO SLIDE—SLIDE. NEVER CHANGE YOUR MIND. It's when you change your mind that trouble starts.

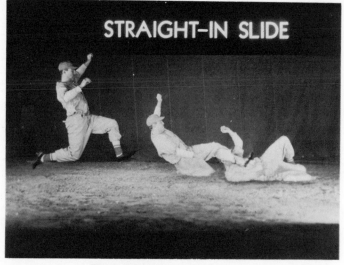

STRAIGHT-IN SLIDE

There are three basic slides. Shown here
is what is known as the straight-in slide.

Approach the bag with your body erect
and your eyes on the bag. Take off for
the slide with whichever foot is most
natural to you. Here the runner is taking
off on his right foot.

Immediately after the take-off, bend the take-off leg under you; raise the other leg well off the ground and extend it toward the bag throwing the upper part of the body backward. Be sure the foot of the bent leg is turned sideways to avoid catching the spikes in the ground.

The bent leg takes the shock of the fall and you slide forward on it until . . .

. . . the extended leg makes contact with the nearest side of the bag.

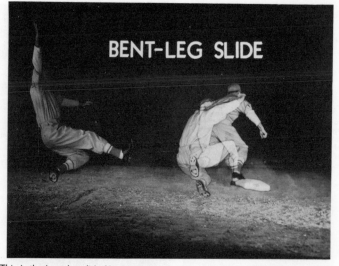

This is the bent-leg slide. Use it to reach the bag and then get back on your feet immediately ready to go on to the next base if you get the chance. The bent-leg slide is very similar to the straight-in slide with these differences—the take-off is closer to the bag; the extended leg is bent slightly more at the knee; and the upper part of the body is more erect.

As your outstretched leg touches the bag, throw your weight upward and forward until you are back on your feet. Then . . .

. . . simply keep on going.

HOOK SLIDE

The hook slide, so called because one
foot hooks the corner of the bag, is used
to avoid being tagged by a fielder covering a base.

Here is the hook slide used in sliding to
the left. This slider has taken off on his
left foot—the foot most natural to him.
In the center action both knees are bent;
both feet are being turned sideways to
avoid catching the spikes in the ground,
the upper part of the body leaning back
and the weight is being thrown to the
slider's left.

The slider hooks the bag with his right foot, thus avoiding the tag.

Here is the hook slide to the right. This runner takes off with his left foot—the natural foot for him. In the action on the right, both knees bend under and the feet are turned sideways, throwing his weight to the right.

The slider hooks the near corner of the bag with his left foot, avoiding the tag.

When holding a base, stand with your left foot touching the inside edge of the base and keep it there until the pitcher assumes his pitching position.

Then take a lead off the base in a direct line with the next base—as long a lead as you dare take, knowing that you can get back safely if necessary.

Stand with your body in good balance, ready to move in either direction quickly. Feet spread, weight slightly forward, ready to start for the next base.

The start for the next base begins by turning the body in the direction of the run.

Then push off with the right foot, and take your first step with your left foot, driving your body along the base line.

Then hustle. Don't let anything stop you from beating out the throw. Make it if it's humanly possible and don't think it's impossible until you've reached the base.

Skill, speed, courage and hustle. That's what makes a good base runner. Good base runners are big factors in winning ball games.

6

PITCHING

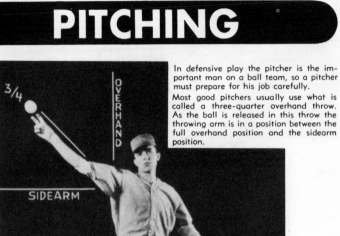

In defensive play the pitcher is the important man on a ball team, so a pitcher must prepare for his job carefully.

Most good pitchers usually use what is called a three-quarter overhand throw. As the ball is released in this throw the throwing arm is in a position between the full overhand position and the sidearm position.

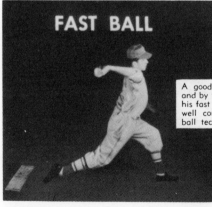

A good pitcher has three basic pitches and by far the most important of these is his fast ball . . . just a fast, straight ball, well controlled. Let's analyze the fast ball technique.

Your grip for the fast ball should be the same every time you throw it. Most good pitchers use this one. First two fingers on top gripping across the seam at the widest spot.

Others grip across the seam at the narrowest spot.

The thumb usually contacts another seam directly underneath the fingers.

As your arm comes forward in the pitch, your upper arm is approximately parallel to the ground and the angle between your upper arm and forearm is approximately a right angle. Your body is erect; your eyes on the target.

When you pitch, the ball should leave your hand approximately beside your head, and this is the crucial part of your pitch. This is where you impart the last ounce of energy for speed—your last chance to give the ball direction.

The last crucial movement of the pitch is a snap of the wrist. Let's practice only this movement first.

To practice the fundamental wrist snap, stand with your upper arm and forearm in that right-angle position and lay your wrist back as far as you can without losing the vertical position of your forearm.

97

Then, throw the ball, using only your wrist and fingers. Let your hand and fingers feel like the tail end of a cracking whip and snap the ball as far and as straight as you can.

Let the ball roll off your fingertips as you release it, and it will leave your hand with an upward spin. That's the wrist snap for the fast ball—one of the most important fundamentals of pitching.

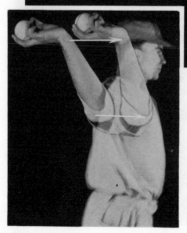

Now let's put some "arm" into the throw. The arm starts to add power at this point, called a layback position.

To practice the arm action, stand with your body comfortably erect and lay your arm back as far as you can with your palm up and your wrist cocked backward.

The elbow leads the forward movement of the throwing arm. Keep your forearm laid back and your wrist cocked, and start your elbow forward. As your elbow comes up even with your shoulder . . .

. . . keep the movement flowing as your forearm comes up to the vertical position.

As the forearm reaches the vertical position, the wrist snaps forward with a decided whipping movement of the hand and fingers.

There is the full arm movement. Practice this movement without moving your body, until it feels perfectly natural to you and you can control your pitches. Then you're ready for the full pitch.

The pitching movement uses every important muscle in your body, starting in your feet and extending progressively through your legs, hips, shoulders and arm, right out to your fingertips. The timing and coordination of all these muscles in a single, smooth, powerful movement makes the difference between a good pitcher and a mediocre one.

This is the forward stance as you wait for the catcher's signal. It is used when it is not necessary to hold men on bases.

In this stance your right foot is on the pitcher's plate with the front spike extended over the front edge. Your left foot is directly behind the plate and all your weight is on your back foot. Keep the ball hidden from the batter.

The pitch starts with a shift of the weight to the forward foot. As you shift, bend forward at the waist and let the arms swing back naturally. At the same time, bend your knees slightly. You MAY shift your rear foot backward. Now reverse the action.

Shift your weight back to the rear foot, straighten up at the waist and start your arms swinging in a low full arc that will finish over your head. The gloved hand comes up in front of the ball.

Swing your arms upward until your hands are comfortably above your head in what is called the stretch position, still keeping your eyes on the target. During this upward swing your right foot turns outward until, at the stretch position, it is almost at a right angle to the direction of your pitch. A slight pause here—and then the pitch.

101

Here is the full pitching movement from the stretch—your body winds back as your arm goes into the layback position. At the same time your body starts forward in a long stride, adding the force of the moving body to the speed of your arm and wrist as they whip the ball through. Then a full follow-through.

The movement starts as you bring your left knee up close across your body and start your throwing arm swinging down and back toward the layback position. At the same time your body pivots around to point your left shoulder at the target.

As your weight shifts onto your right foot, push off with that foot, launching your body in the direction of the pitch. At the same time . . .

. . . stride forward, directly toward the plate, with your cocked left leg, bringing your throwing arm to the layback position. Now your body is moving forward fast.

As soon as the left foot touches the ground, start uncoiling your body. The weight is now on your left foot. The hips and shoulders pivot around square with the plate.

At the same time start your throwing arm whipping through toward the release point. The elbow is now leading the arm movement.

Release the ball with a snap of the wrist. Thus, as the ball is released, everything is moving forward—body, shoulder, arm, hand and right foot . . .

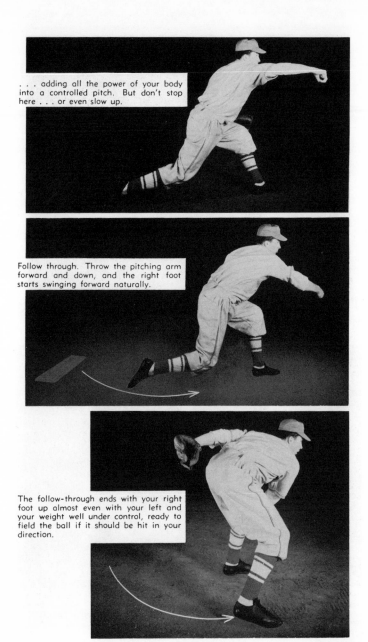

. . . adding all the power of your body into a controlled pitch. But don't stop here . . . or even slow up.

Follow through. Throw the pitching arm forward and down, and the right foot starts swinging forward naturally.

The follow-through ends with your right foot up almost even with your left and your weight well under control, ready to field the ball if it should be hit in your direction.

There is the complete pitching movement. One — weight forward. Two — weight back for the stretch. Three—knee cocked and everything coiled back. Four—the stride and Five—the pitch . . . everything smoothly, powerfully uncoiled in a whip-like action that starts in the rear foot, travels through your body and arm and ends in the follow-through.

When it's necessary to hold a runner or runners on base, you will have to use this sideward stance and a slightly different sequence of movement in your pitch. In the sideward stance the right foot is against the front of the rubber and your left is a comfortable distance ahead. Your weight rests evenly on both feet. From this position you may raise your arms overhead first.

Then drop your hands down into a resting position close to your body, your
arms relaxed against the sides of your
body, the ball in contact with your throwing hand and your glove.

The position of the feet may be in the
open stance with the left foot slightly
toward first base, as in the picture on

the left, or in the parallel stance as in
the picture on the right. The open stance
is commonly used to hold a runner on
first base. The closed stance is most
commonly used to hold a man on second,
although many good pitchers use several
variations of this principle.

To start the pitch from the sideward
stance, don't cock your knee. Simply
shift your weight back to the right foot
and let your pitching arm swing back

into the layback position. From there
your stride is straight forward toward the
plate . . . long and low. The knee cock is
practically eliminated.

After the stride the arm and body movements are exactly the same as in the pitch from the forward stance. The first requirement of any pitcher is a well controlled fast ball from both the forward and sideward stance. After you have mastered that pitch you can go on to the curve and change of pace.

CURVE BALL

A curve is a pitch in which you give the ball a spin that makes it change direction as it nears the plate. To throw a curve you follow the same basic fundamentals that you use in your fast ball with two exceptions—the grip and the action of hand and wrist on delivery.

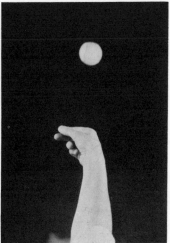

Your grip is similar to the fast ball grip, except that you exert considerably more pressure with the second finger than with the index finger.

And as you deliver the ball you twist your hand inward from the wrist at the same time as the wrist snap. The ball rolls off the outside of your first finger, thus developing the spin that makes it change direction on its way to the plate.

CHANGE OF PACE

The change-of-pace ball is pitched with a delivery that looks like a fast ball, but it travels more slowly.

Some pitchers grip the ball loosely well back in the hand for a change of pace ball and deliver it with very little pressure by the fingers—somewhat like a shot-put delivery.

Others keep the normal grip and achieve the change of pace through the action of their fingers as they release the ball.

Just as they release the ball they relax their fingers, thus taking some of the speed off the ball.

The fast ball, the curve and the change of pace, once mastered with speed and control, provide variety enough for good defensive baseball. Practice them well and study your movement constantly to make sure it contains all the fundamentals and you are well on your way to successful pitching.

7

CATCHING

In every baseball game the catcher is the key strategist of defensive play.

The catcher's position should be as close as possible to the batter without interfering with him. In this position he is able to present a better target to the pitcher and, close to the plate, he can handle low pitches and foul tips better.

While giving signals to the pitcher, the catcher should be in a squat position, feet comfortably apart, knees turned out, left forearm resting on the thigh.

The gloved hand extends beyond the left knee. The throwing hand gives the signal in the crotch or inside the legs.

As soon as the signal for the pitch is given, raise up a little from the squat position and take a comfortable stance with your feet well spread apart . . . the right foot slightly behind the left.

Your throwing hand should be relaxed and the fingers closed loosely around your thumb. Don't clench your fist; just let your thumb relax behind your index finger.

Don't change the position of your hands until after the pitcher has started his delivery. If the pitch is below the waist, your gloved hand should be held out with the palm toward the pitcher, fingers pointing down.

If the pitch is above the waist, the fingers of your gloved hand should point upward.

To catch the ball, you simply roll your right hand around to the front of the glove and trap the ball in the pocket.

As the right hand swings over to hold the ball, the fingers automatically encircle the ball in the correct throwing position.

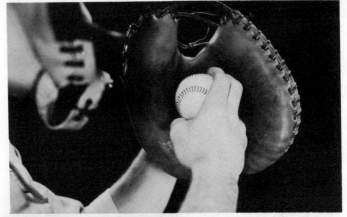

In throwing, a catcher should use a snap overhand throw whenever possible. It gets the ball away faster.

Here is your fastest throwing action. The same snap overhand throw you learned earlier from the throwing unit of this series. From the receiving position get your arm, body and feet into the layback position the shortest possible way. Avoid the full swing if possible. It wastes time and may hurry you to the point where you sacrifice control.

From the layback position make a snap overhand throw with all your power. One of the most important requirements of a good catcher is that he must be able to throw.

But throwing presents special problems to a catcher because he usually has a batter in front of him to obstruct his throw. To get around the batter there are certain fundamental movements in a catcher's footwork. Here are some of the more complicated movements.

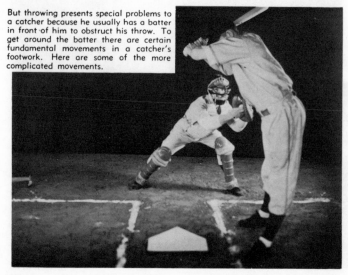

If you have a right-handed batter at the plate and the pitch is outside—to your right—here is your footwork for a throw.

From your catching position you step to the right with the right foot to catch the ball. This takes you clear of the batter.

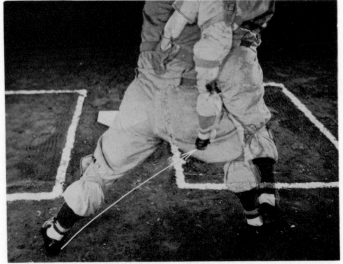

From that position you can take one step forward with the left foot and throw. There is the footwork for a throw to the right, with an outside pitch and a right handed batter. First, a step to the right with the right foot to catch the ball. Then forward with the left foot for the throw.

With a right-handed batter and an inside pitch a different pattern of footwork is required for the throw.

First, step to the left to make the catch, then to the right with the right foot, then forward with the left to throw.

If you have a right-handed batter and an inside pitch and you want to throw to third base, the batter is very much. in your way. Here's your footwork to avoid him.

Take a step to the left with the left foot
to get into position for the catch.

Then, with the right foot, step diagonally
left and back until your right foot is behind your left. This takes you clear of
the batter.

Then step toward third with your left foot
and throw behind the hitter.

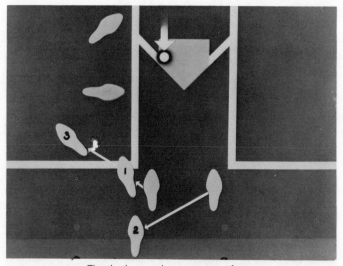

There's the complete movement, for a
throw to third with a right-handed batter
and an inside pitch. Step left to make
the catch, then diagonally back and left
with the right foot, then toward third
with the left foot to make the throw.

With a left-handed batter and an inside pitch a throw to second base requires a specific footwork pattern to avoid the batter.

A step to the right with the right foot puts you in position for the catch. From here, shift your weight back to the left foot.

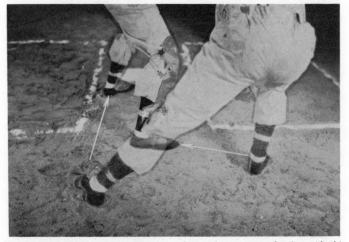

Then, in quick succession, a step diagonally forward and to the left with the right foot and a forward step toward second base with the left for the throw.

As you become more familiar with this footwork the last two steps will become a jump shift—a 1-2 count instead of a 1-2-3 count.

119

For a throw to second from an outside pitch to a left-handed hitter, there is the first move. Step left to catch the ball first.

Then swing your right foot diagonally back behind the left as you lay back for the throw.

Then step forward with the left foot and throw.

On a throw to first base, you can step behind the batter, as shown here. If the pitch is to the outside the catcher may throw in front of the batter.

Among other things, a catcher has to handle many fly balls. The first thing he must do is flip off his mask and toss it in the direction opposite to the ball. Then he must get under the ball fast and wait for it, remembering . . .

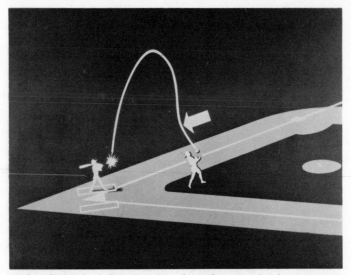

. . . the infield drift. A fly ball in the home plate area has a strong spin toward the infield. As the ball comes down, it will break toward the infield. Therefore the catcher must adjust his waiting position accordingly. Here a catcher waits for a fly ball in front of the plate, playing it over his head.

A catcher handles many bunts too. He should start immediately for any bunt in his area.

If the bunted ball is rolling, place your glove in front of it and scoop it into your mitt with your throwing hand.

If it has stopped rolling, you may pick it up with your throwing hand only on a fast play, but two hands should be used whenever possible.

In a force play at home plate, that is, if a runner from third base is being forced home and it is not necessary to tag him, stand with your left foot on the front of the plate, facing in the direction of the throw.

Keep your left foot on the plate and step forward with your right foot as you receive the ball. Then to complete the double play . . .

. . . pivot on the right foot and throw to first base.

Covering home plate in defensive play, a catcher should know the technique of tagging a runner. To tag a runner coming into the plate, first place yourself in a position facing the throw.

To tag him, drop low, holding the ball firmly with both hands, the back of the glove toward the incoming runner. Never tag a runner with only one hand unless it is the only possible way to get him in time.

Another very important part of a catcher's job has nothing to do with technique. He is the only player who faces all the others, and he is the defensive strategist in emergencies. So to him falls the job of maintaining much of the team's morale. He should be full of pep and enthusiasm, and, at the same time, calm enough to make sound decisions quickly.

Catching is a big part of baseball. A player who wants to be a catcher should learn the fundamental skills of the position thoroughly—practice them until they are instinctive because, as the team's strategist, he'll have other things to think of during a game.

LEARN TO KEEP A SCORECARD

The ability to keep an accurate record of the play-by-play action of a baseball game adds much to the enjoyment of watching and playing the game. Keeping score is easily done by using numbers and abbreviations to identify the players and their actions during the game:

SCORECARD

WOLVES	AB	R	H	E	RBI
EGAN 4	4	1	3	0	2
JONES 7	4	1	1	0	1
BUTZ 6	5	1	0	0	0
GEORGE 3	5	0	2	0	2
COX 5	3	3	2	0	0
BRADY 8	5	1	2	0	0
Mitchell 9	5	0	1	0	1
GIBBONS 2	5	0	1	0	2
WINSLOW 1	0	1	0	0	0
SMITH 5th	—	0	0	0	0
COLT 6th	—	0	0	0	0
HANSEN 8th	—	1	1	0	0
CLARK 9th	0	0	0	0	0
RUNS - HITS / ERROR - LEFT	39	9	13	0	8

POSITION NUMBERS OF PLAYERS

1—Pitcher	4—2nd Baseman	7—Left Fielder
2—Catcher	5—3rd Baseman	8—Center Fielder
3—1st Baseman	6—Shortstop	9—Right Fielder

ACTION DURING PLAY

W—Walk	PB—Passed Ball	AB—Times at Bat
K—Strike Out	WP—Wild Pitch	R—Runs
E—Error	HP—Hit by Pitch	H—Hits
B—Balk	DP—Double Play	RBI—Runs Batted in
O—Out	TP—Triple Play	g—Ground Ball (for
F—Foul Out	S—Stolen Base	unassisted infield
FO—Force Out	OS—Out Stealing	outs)
H—Sacrifice	FC—Fielder's Choice	(number) — the num-
		ber of the defensive
		player who makes a
		put-out, assist, or er-
		ror.

You will notice on the scorecard that the batter's progress around the bases is indicated by diagonal lines within his own inning-square. Each line represents one base (marked in a clockwise direction). Above each line is a small letter or number which explains how the batter or runner moved to that particular base, or, in the case of a batter making a hit, to what field the ball travelled. Succeeding numbers then show either the number of the team-mate who moved him to the next base or bases, or the letter describing another reason for his advance.

For instance, the first batter in the 6th inning, Cox, got to first base on a single (one diagonal line) to center field (8). He stole (S) second base. He went to third on what Mitchell (9) did, and scored on what Gibbons (2) did.

Extra base hits are indicated by diagonal lines equal to the number of bases made. For example, the first batter in the 7th inning hit a home-run, shown by four lines to all four bases. In the third inning, Jones got a double, shown by two lines to second base.

THE PLAY-BY-PLAY

(See Scorecard)

First Inning: Egan (2b) struck out. Jones (lf) grounded out, second baseman to first. Butz (ss) flied out to left field.

Second Inning: George (1b) fouled out to the catcher. Cox (3b) walked. Brady (cf) singled to right field, sending Cox to third base. Mitchell (rf) flied out to center, Cox scoring after the catch. Gibbons (c) grounded out, shortstop to first.

Third Inning: Winslow (p) was hit by a pitch ball and took first base. Egan sacrificed Winslow to second, and was thrown out, third baseman to first. Jones doubled to right field, scoring

Winslow from second. Butz flied out to right field. George singled to left, scoring Jones from second. George stole second base. Cox grounded out to the first baseman, unassisted.

Fourth Inning: Brady grounded out, shortstop to first after the pitcher deflected the ball for an assist. Mitchell singled to right. Gibbons hit into a double play, shortstop to second base to first, Mitchell being forced at second.

Fifth Inning: Smith batted for the pitcher Winslow and lined out to the third baseman. Egan singled to left, Jones walked, moving Egan to second. Butz was safe on a fielder's choice when the pitcher took his grounder and threw to the third baseman for a force-out on Egan, Jones taking second on the play. Jones and Butz advanced to third and second on a wild pitch. George grounded to the first baseman who threw to the pitcher covering first base for the third out. Colt came in to pitch.

Sixth Inning: Cox singled to center. Brady fouled out to the second baseman. Cox stole second base. Mitchell was safe on an error by the second baseman, Cox taking third on the play. Gibbons flied out to right, Cox scoring from third after the catch. Colt grounded to the shortstop, who elected to throw to the second baseman for a force-out on Mitchell to retire the side.

Seventh Inning: Egan hit a home-run over the right field fence. Jones grounded out, pitcher to first. Butz went all the way to second base when the left fielder dropped his fly ball. George singled to right, scoring Butz. George went to second on a balk. Cox walked. Brady was safe on a fielder's choice when the catcher took his short grounder and threw to the third baseman for a force-out on George. Mitchell rolled out, shortstop to first.

Eighth Inning: Gibbons singled to center. Gibbons tried to steal second and was thrown out, catcher to second baseman. Hansen batted for the pitcher Colt and doubled to left. Egan singled to right, scoring Hansen from second. Egan took second on a wild pitch. Jones fouled out to the third baseman. Butz flied out to left.

Ninth Inning: George struck out. Cox singled to right. Brady singled to center, Cox taking third. Mitchell was safe on a fielder's choice when the pitcher took his grounder and, trying for a double play, threw wildly to second base, Cox scoring on the error and Brady going all the way to third. Gibbons flied to center, Brady scoring after the catch. (In this example, this last run broke a tie game in the last of the ninth.)